home body

home body

rupi kaur

Andrews McMeel
PUBLISHING®

the
foreword

i write because i can't live without it.

i write because i am homesick for a place i've
never been.

i write because it's the only way i know how to feel
close to myself.

and these poems—

these poems. happen to me. they don't listen to my
instructions. they don't care for deadlines, or rules, or
any pressures i may put on them. the poems cook and
cook and cook inside my body until they're ready. the
ingredients are found in the conversations i hear and
live. the ideas marinate.

the poems bubble and bubble and bubble until there
is no room left inside me. that bubbling is one of the
most glorious feelings i've ever felt. it's like the rush of
joy you'd feel after winning a race. i could be taking a
shower, having a conversation, or lying in bed at 2 a.m.,
and suddenly a poem is rising up my belly—past my
chest—up my throat—onto my lips—and i'm running
and running and running to catch it with a piece of paper
before it escapes me.

i began writing *home body* while fighting one of
the most difficult battles of my life. an unforgiving
depression was draining me of my vitality and spirit.

i felt like i was dying from the inside. as if i were frozen in place and the world was moving on without me. as the years passed, i lost more and more will to live.

this book is proof that i won a battle i thought was going to kill me. above all, i'm excited to take *home body* into the future, because waiting inside tomorrow are bigger battles. and when i fight them, i won't be wondering whether i'm going to make it. i know that i will, because these poems are a testament to my survival.

home body is about what broke me and what put me back together. i wrote while getting help. i wrote while getting better. i wrote on days when i couldn't make it out of bed. i wrote on days when i rejoiced in the company of friends. i wrote when i hurt and when i cried. i wrote when i found laughter again. i wrote about the support of sisters. i wrote when the world burned from the fires of injustice. i wrote about the hope given to me by my community. i wrote when i saw my parents getting tossed out by a world that valued them solely for their labor. i wrote during a global pandemic. i wrote about honoring my mind and body so i could wake up and help build a world that serves all people.

home body is how i taught myself to thunder, roar, and shine.

after feeling disconnected for so long
my mind and body are finally
coming back to each other

- *home body*

contents

mind

i'm in the darkest room of my life

maybe i walked out of the womb with it
is it possible to be born
with such a melancholy spirit
maybe it met me at the airport
slid into my passport
and remained with me
long after we landed in
a country that did not want us
maybe it was on my father's face
when he met us in baggage claim
and i had no idea who he was
maybe the rapist left it behind
or was it that criminal i called a boyfriend
maybe he beat it into me
maybe i met the one
and lost him
maybe it was the love
of my life's parting gift
or maybe
it was all of those things at once

- *where the depression came from*

why do i let my mind
get under my skin
i am so sensitive

my mind keeps running off to dark corners
and coming back with reasons for
why i am not enough

sex is a way for people to
transcend into each other
and come apart
a beautiful earthy expression
but for me
sex was my girlhood
dragged to death
he said
we were going to play
then he always locked the door
always chose the game
when i told him to stop
he said i was asking for it
but what did i know
about involuntary orgasms
and agency
and consent
at age 7. 8. 9. and 10.

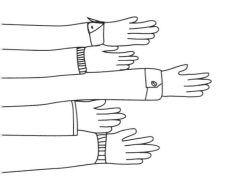

i'll be quiet when
we can say *sexual assault*
and they
stop screaming *liar*

depression is silent
you never hear it coming
and suddenly it's
the loudest voice in your head

my mind
my body
and i
all live in one place
but it feels like we are
three completely different people

- *disconnected*

while everyone else
was living their life in color
depression froze me in place

nothing lasts forever
let that be the reason you stay
even this sick twisted misery
will not last

- *hope*

i have never known anything more
quietly loud than anxiety

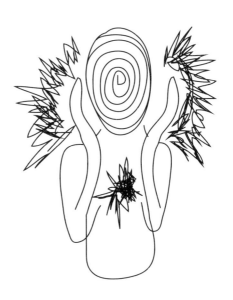

if you could accept
that perfection is impossible
what would you stop obsessing over

you are lonely
but you are not alone

- there is a difference

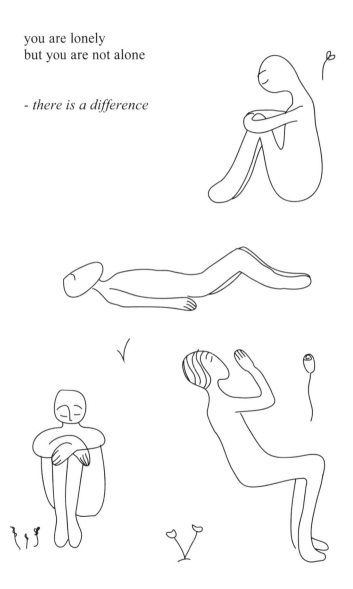

it feels like i'm watching my life happen through
a fuzzy television screen. i feel far away from this
world. almost foreign in this body. as if every happy
memory has been wiped clean from the bowl of my
mind. i close my eyes and i can't remember what
happy feels like. my chest collapses into my stomach
knowing that i have to get up in the morning and
pretend i'm not fading away all over again. i want
to reach out and touch things. i want to feel them
touch me back. i want to live. i want the vitality of
my life back.

abuse doesn't just happen
in romantic relationships
abuse can live
in friendships too

i walked offstage
once the show was over
and prayed for the misery to
stop eating me alive
i was sick
and pretending not to be sick
at least performing kept me moving
coming home to an
empty apartment was worse
without work i had nothing to look forward to
i'd sink into the depression for months
half passed out from the grief
eyes open
mind lost in another dimension
write the book they said
get back on the road again
what's taking you so long

- *empty*

i want to live
i'm just afraid
i won't measure up to the
idea people have of me in their heads
i'm afraid of getting older
scared i'll never write anything
worth reading again
that i'll disappoint the people
who are counting on me
that i'll never learn how to be happy
that i'll be broke again one day
that my parents will die
and i'll be alone in the end

being molested as a child has been the most confusing
experience of my life. to learn sex without having any
concept of it has messed me up in more ways than
i'm aware of. to feel an orgasm so young. to have my
life threatened. to be stretched. bruised. bit. spit on.
to become a woman at the age of four. to know fear
intimately. have it breathe down my neck. to be numb.
stiff. silent. and own all the world's shame at once.

the need to survive
lit a fire in me

i want to be snapped
cracked
hammered into
i want to open where i am closed
find the secret door
let me out of me
i want something to
hold me by the neck
split me down the middle
and make me feel alive again

- *i don't want to be numb anymore*

i am trusting the uncertainty
and believing i will
end up somewhere
right and good

there is nothing wrong with you
this is growth
this is transformation
protecting yourself
getting lost in the noise
figuring it out
feeling used
uncared for
losing hope
burning out
this is fear
this is processing
this is surviving
this is being alive

- *journey*

you lose everything
when you don't love yourself

- and gain everything when you do

i am not my worst days
i am not what happened to me

- *reminder*

there are whole blackouts
in some of the years i have lived
my therapist says our minds erase trauma
to help us move on
but every experience i've had
is memorized in my flesh
even if my mind forgets
my body remembers
my body is the map of my life
my body wears what it's been through
my body signals the alarms when
it thinks danger is coming
and suddenly
the hungry little demons from my past
come raging out of my flesh
screaming
don't you forget us
don't you ever try to
leave us behind again

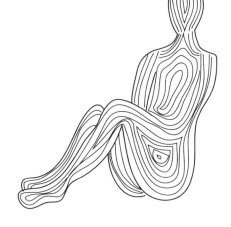

i'm either romanticizing the past
or i'm busy worrying about the future
it's no wonder
i don't feel alive
i'm not living
in the only moment that's real

- *present*

anxiety feels like i'm hanging
off the side of a building
and my hand is going to
slip any second

how can i be so
cruel to myself
when i'm doing the best i can

- *be gentle*

list of things to heal your mood:

1) cry it. walk it. write it. scream it. dance it
   out of your body.
2) if after all that
   you are still
   spiraling out of control
   ask yourself if sinking into the mud is worth it
3) the answer is no
4) the answer is breathe
5) sip tea and feel your nervous system settle
6) you are the hero of your life
7) this feeling doesn't have power over you
8) the universe has prepared you to handle this
9) no matter how dark it gets
   the light is always on its way
10) you are the light
11) walk yourself back to where the love lives

i am not broken
because of the depression
i am not a lesser version of myself
because of the anxiety
i am a whole
complete
and complicated person

- *full*

i am loving myself out of the dark

i'm breathing aren't i
that's gotta be a sign that
the universe is on my side
if i've made it this far
i can make it all the way

imagine what we could accomplish if
we didn't have to spend our energy
protecting ourselves from
society's rapist problem

most of my life has been spent
with the two of us touching
skin to skin
our nights together
and sometimes our days
you carried me when my limbs refused to
when i was so sick i could not move
not once did you tire of my weight
not once did you complain
you've witnessed all my dreams
my sex
my writing
my weeping
every vulnerable act of my life
has been with you
the two of us knee-deep in laughter
and when i've been a fool to trust a fool
made love on top of you
left for days only to
return empty-handed
you always took me back
when sleep abandoned me
we lay awake together
you are the embrace of my life
my confessional
my altar
i went from girl to woman on top of you
and in the end
it will be you—old friend
delivering me to death well rested

- there is no place more intimate than a bed

you didn't lose it
happiness has always been here

- *you just lost perspective*

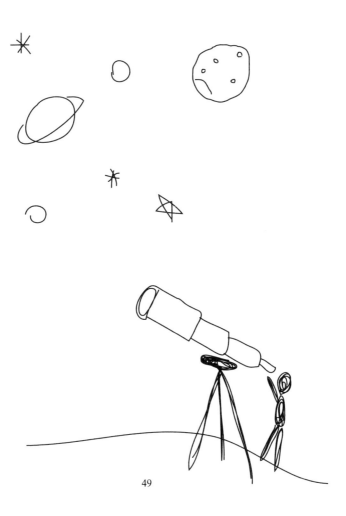

what we lived through
is living in us

i am not a victim of my life
what i went through
pulled a warrior out of me
and it is my greatest honor to be her

for the love of my life
i am trying my best to have hope
i'll keep greeting each morning
with an *i will*
when it feels like i can't
i will
i will
i will
meet a day that will melt me
i will move and the sadness *will*
fall off my shoulders
to make room for joy
i will be full of color
i will touch the sky again

i want a parade
i want music
i want confetti
i want a marching band
for the ones surviving in silence
i want a standing ovation
for every person who
wakes up and moves toward the sun
when there is a shadow
pulling them back on the inside

our pain is the doorway to our joy

i'm tired of being disappointed
in the home that keeps me alive
i'm exhausted by the energy it takes
to hate myself

- i'm putting the hate down

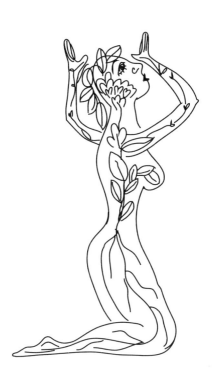

heart

sometimes
i love you means
i want to love you

sometimes
i love you means
i'll stay a little while longer

sometimes
i love you means
i'm not sure how to leave

sometimes
i love you means
i have nowhere else to go

i have difficulty separating
abusive relationships
from healthy ones
i can't tell the difference
between love and violence

- *it all looks the same*

i was trying to make him the one
and it took me three years to realize
love doesn't work like that

men like him are experts at
smelling out girls like me
the invisible ones
who believe they must be ugly
because their fathers didn't love them
he said my name
and i had never heard my name
dance off a man's lips before
give a little attention
to someone who's never had any
and they'll be slipping and falling
all over the place
unable to contain the joy
of being wanted
the relief of being discovered
he groomed me into thinking
i couldn't survive without him
this is how men like him
trap girls like me

- *predator*

don't ask me why i didn't leave
he made my world so small
i couldn't see the exit

- *i'm surprised i got out at all*

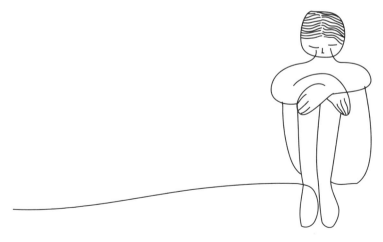

if someone doesn't have a heart
you can't go around
offering them yours

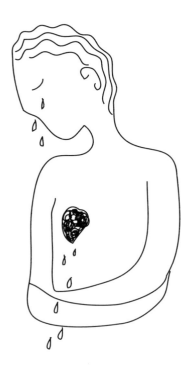

each time i showed you a piece of heaven
it was a warning
every stroll we took
through the garden of my life
all the flowers that bloomed for you
the peacocks that sang your name
were a sign
yet
after seeing all my magic
you hit your head and lost it
went and scattered yourself across this town
thinking if you were lucky enough to taste me
you'd get your hands on something better
everything dulled in comparison
now you're back
body spilling all over my floor
begging me
to crush you with my thighs
pull you into my hips
transcend you to heaven with my pussy
i had you on the greatest trip of your life
i had you seeing visions
each time i showed you a piece of heaven
every stroll we took through the garden of my life
all the flowers that bloomed for you
the peacocks that sang your name
were a sign of all you'd lose
if you betrayed me

- *consequences*

if you're waiting for them
to make you feel like you're enough
you'll be waiting a long time

i'm leaving
cause i'm not happy here
i don't want to reach the end of my life
still having doubts about
the man i've been with
since my twenties

why does everything
become less beautiful
once it belongs to us

it took me getting into a healthy relationship
to realize i shouldn't be scared
of the person i love

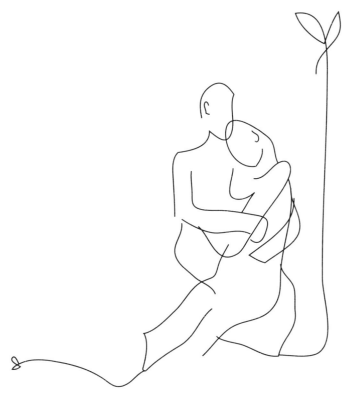

i used to cry
because i could not find
a good man to love me
now i have one and
he isn't enough
the others were always
halfway out the door

- that's what made them alluring

why do i hurt the ones
who want to lift me up and
worship the ones who crush me

- *what made me like this*

i don't know what to do with a man
who wants to hold on to me
for the rest of our lives

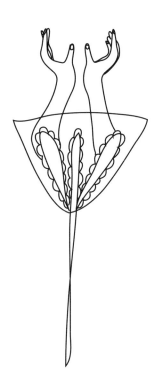

i'm afraid i won't find the one who sees me
and rushes to breathe me in
i have a fear of seeming too desperate
i'm scared i will be cheated on
with a woman more brilliant
more striking
more of me in every way
terrified this will confirm what i know already
that i am not enough for someone to stay
where is the burning match that will set me on fire
what if i've already walked by the one
on a street corner
what if i've already been with them
and ruined it
who will love me enough to
spend their energy getting close
to someone so inconsistent
what if the one i want
is someone who touches me and leaves
and the one who doesn't leave
is someone i can't stand touching me
will it always be bad timing
will i ever be sure
will i settle
will i be on my own forever

your partner is supposed to
enrich your life
not drain it
staying when it hurts is not love

i'm too in love with my life
to be spilling all over the floor
for the next man
who gives me butterflies
when i could look in the mirror
and take my own breath away

the love of family
friends and community
is just as potent
as the love
of a romantic relationship

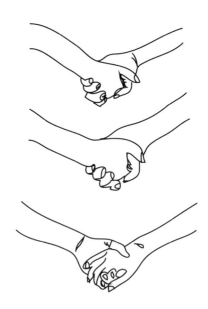

nothing can replace
how the women in my life
make me feel

it's impossible
for one person to
fill you up
in all the ways
you need to be filled
your partner
can't be your everything

i can live without romantic love
but i can't survive without
the women i call friends
they know exactly what i need
before i even know i need it
the way we hold space
for each other is just different

a man can't give me anything
i can't give myself

- *things i wish i could tell the younger me*

masturbation
is meditation

in a world that doesn't consider
my body to be mine
self-pleasure is an act
of self-preservation
when i'm feeling disconnected
i connect with my center
touch by touch
i drop back into myself
at the orgasm

i'm not going to pretend
to be less intelligent than i am
so a man can feel
more comfortable around me
the one i deserve
will see my greatness and
want to lift it higher

i want you to wipe away
everything you know about love
and start with one word
kindness
give it to them
let them give it to you
be two pillars
equal in your love
and you'll carry empires on your backs

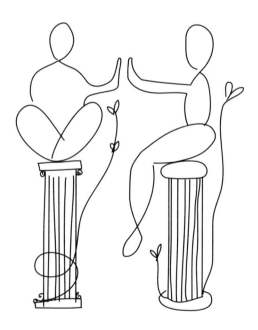

i wrap my holy legs
around his heavy head
and let his tongue swim
toward salvation

- *baptize*

i want someone who is
inspired by my brilliance
not threatened by it

look me in the eyes
when you're down there
eating for your life

- *i want you to see what you do to me*

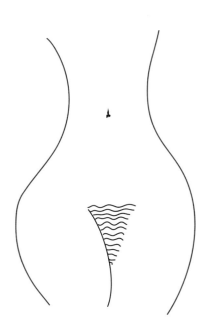

i'm careful about
who i spend my energy on

- i know my worth

my body is so hot from wanting you
i'm spilling by the time we take our clothes off
i want the kind of love that
transcends me
into another realm
i want you so deep
we enter the spirit world
go from being gentle to rough
i want eye contact
spread my legs to
opposite ends of the room
and look with your fingers
i want my soul to be touched
by the tip of yours
i want to come
out of this room
different people

- *can you do that*

rest

there are years in me
that have not slept

i measure my self-worth
by how productive i've been
but no matter
how hard i work
i still feel inadequate

- *productivity guilt*

i fear that
my best years are behind me
and nothing beyond this point will add up

productivity

anxiety

i have this productivity anxiety
that everyone else is working harder than me
and i'm going to be left behind
cause i'm not working fast enough
long enough
and i'm wasting my time

i don't sit down to have breakfast
i take it to go
i call my mother when i'm free—otherwise
it takes too long to have a conversation

i put off everything that
won't bring me closer to my dreams
as if the things i'm putting off
are not the dream themselves

isn't the dream
that i have a mother to call
and a table to eat breakfast at

instead i'm lost in the sick need
to optimize every hour of my day
so i'm improving in some way
making money in some way
advancing my career in some way
because that's what it takes
to be successful
right

i excavate my life
package it up
sell it to the world
and when they ask for more
i dig through bones
trying to write poems

capitalism got inside my head
and made me think my only value
is how much i produce
for people to consume
capitalism got inside my head
and made me think
i am of worth
as long as i am working

i learned impatience from it
i learned self-doubt from it
learned to plant seeds in the ground
and expect flowers the next day

but magic
doesn't work like that
magic doesn't happen
cause i've figured out how to
pack more work in a day
magic moves
by the laws of nature
and nature has its own clock
magic happens
when we play
when we escape
daydream and imagine
that's where everything
with the power to fulfill us
is waiting on its knees for us

- productivity anxiety

we can work
at our own pace
and still be
successful

a
lifetime
on the road

while i was growing up
my dad worked six days a week
driving an eighteen-wheeler truck
from one end of the continent to the other

he'd come home
after a week on the road
while my siblings and i would be sleeping
the sound of the front door always woke me
the basement we lived in was small
i could hear mom in the kitchen
making him a fresh meal of dal and roti

dad would eat
shower
settle into bed
but as soon as his eyes drifted off
his boss would call and say

get back on the road again
and just like that
we'd catch a glimpse of dad leaving

when you're an immigrant
you keep your head down and stay working
when you're a refugee and
you don't have papers
when they call you illegal
outsider
terrorist
towelhead
you work until your bones become dust
you are the only one you can count on

every time he started at a new company
he'd spend months working for free
during their mandatory "training" period
funny how they needed to train a man
who was fully licensed
qualified
and experienced

after the third month of
not taking a penny home
dad would demand compensation
and they'd offer him
five cents for every mile he drove

years ago while driving a load
from montreal to florida
he ended up at a hospital

somewhere in the middle of america
with his appendix moments away
from bursting

when the doctor told him
they had to get him into surgery immediately
he looked at her and said
i can't afford it
can this wait until i get back home to canada

when do you get back home the doctor asked

in three days he responded
and she looked at him like he must
be out of his mind

luckily
she didn't have it in her
to let him risk his life
she performed the surgery for free that night
and you want to know what my dad did
right after they stitched him up
he walked out of the hospital
climbed into his truck
finished the delivery
and spent three days driving back home

why would you put yourself through that i ask
he shrugs his shoulders and tells me
my boss wouldn't get me a flight home
where would i leave my truck

i couldn't drive back with a trailer full
of undelivered car parts
and risk losing my job

while listening to him
all i can think is that
no one should have to work to the bone like that
it breaks me into pieces to hear
about every person who grinds
for less than what they're worth
how do we sleep at night
knowing the systems we uphold
treat the foundations of our society
as second-class citizens
when they are the reason
the wheels of this world stay turning

i want to give my dad
a lifetime of peace
for the lifetime he spent
on the road to feed us
i want him to know
what comfort feels like
i want him to see
he's done enough

- a lifetime on the road

when the kids at school asked
where my mom worked
i lied and said *at the factory*
like all the other moms
i was too embarrassed to admit
she didn't have a "real job"
even though "stay-at-home mom" meant
she was a full-time caregiver
driver
chef
secretary
tutor
cleaner
best friend
of four kids and
the world's definition of a "real job"
couldn't begin to cover all that

- *value*

we were always in survival mode
long after we didn't need to be

- *habit*

i'm stuck in
this constant cycle
of running off to build my life
and running back cause
i feel guilty about not
spending enough time with them

- *parent-guilt*

i thought my brown immigrant body
should always work harder
than everyone else in the room
because that's what made me valuable

our elders are not disposable

the land sprawled its limbs
and said *put your feet up*
the trees said *we will give you life*
the air said *breathe me in*
the earth said
take care of what takes care of you
and we turned our backs on all of them

- betrayal

we've ruined
our only home for
convenience and profit
neither of which will be
useful once the earth
can't breathe

being the loudest on earth's playground
doesn't make us any more important than
the dirt we crush beneath our feet
we are nothing except air
and fire and water and soil
we are a people
who forget what we are made of
a people who talk about the weather
as if it's mundane and not magic
as if the oceans
are not holy water
as if the sky
is not a vision
as if the animals
are not our siblings
as if nature is not god
and rain is not god's tears
and we are not god's children
as if god is not the earth itself

i was trying to fit into a system
that left me empty

- *capitalism*

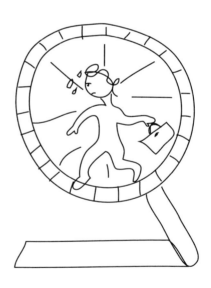

i thought i could
accomplish my way
into being happy
but nothing on the outside
fulfilled me in the ways
it had promised

happiness grew old
waiting for me
and i grew old
searching for happiness
in places it did not live

our souls
will not be soothed
by what we achieve
how we look
or all the hard work we do
even if we managed to
make all the money in the world
we'd be left feeling empty for something
our souls ache for community
our deepest being craves one another
we need to be connected
to feel alive

i get so lost
in where i want to go
i forget that the place i'm in
is already quite magical

i miss the days my friends
knew every mundane detail about my life
and i knew every ordinary detail about theirs
adulthood has starved me of that consistency
that *us*
the walks around the block
the long conversations when we were
too lost in the moment to care what time it was
when we won and celebrated
when we failed and celebrated harder
when we were *just kids*
now we have our very important jobs
that fill up our very busy schedules
we compare calendars just to plan coffee dates
that one of us eventually cancels
cause adulthood is being too exhausted
to leave our apartments most days
i miss knowing i once belonged
to a group of people bigger than myself
that belonging made life easier to live

- *friendship nostalgia*

we already have the things that can complete us
they just aren't things
they are people
and laughter and connection

- *irreplaceable*

you might have done
the external work
but your mind is starving
for internal attention

- listen

i'm throwing the whole concept of
commercialized self-help out altogether
i'm tired of buying products and services
that don't make me feel any better

- *empty promises*

i don't care about perfection
i'd rather roll deep
in the messiness of life

we think we are lost
while our fuller
found and complete selves
are somewhere in the future
we get on our hands and knees
thinking self-improvement will
help us reach them
but this finding ourselves bullshit
is never going to end
i'm tired of putting off living until
i have more information on who i am
i'm a new person every month
always becoming and unbecoming
only to become again
our fuller selves are not off in the future
they're right here
in the only moment that exists
i don't need fixing
i will be searching for answers my whole life
not because i'm a half-formed thing
but because i'm brilliant enough to keep growing
everything necessary to live a vivid life
already exists in me

- i am complete simply because i am imperfect

productivity is not how much
work i do in a day
but how well i balance
what i need to stay healthy

- *being productive is knowing when to rest*

i have to honor my mind and body
if i want to sustain this journey

- *life*

no one is qualified to decide your worth
you wake up and live your life every day
yours is the only opinion of you
that matters

little poet
it seems like the more words you write
the more you think
it is you writing them
why do you think you're in control
didn't the words come spilling
out of you the first time
pouring without permission
and now you're trying to
make them work for you
but magic doesn't move like that
your rushing is
suffocating the masterpieces
baking inside you
your job is to
show up for the process
be patient and when it's time
the universe will use you again

- *inspiration*

if you tried
and didn't end up
where you wanted to go
that's still progress

quiet down i begged my mind
your overthinking is
robbing us of joy

not everything you do has
to be self-improving
you are not a machine
you are a person
without rest
your work can never be full
without play
your mind can never be nourished

- *balance*

play is when we escape time

if you want to be creative
you need to learn how to
do stuff that has no purpose
art isn't made by
working all the time
first you've got to
go out and live

- the art will come

get out of your own way
get out of your own way
get out of your own way

i'm done trying to
prove myself
to myself

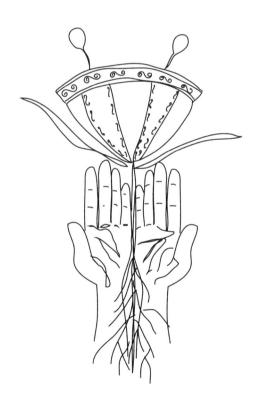

i became confident
once i decided that having fun
was far more important than
my fear of looking silly

- *dancing in public*

we've worked so hard
to be here
we can afford to
slow down and enjoy the view

awake

i'm waking up
from the longest night of my life
it's been years since i've seen the sun

- *awakening*

you can't quiet a woman who was born muzzled

i fell from the mouth of my mother's legs
into the palms of this world
with god herself raging in me

- *birth*

i paid in blood to be here. i paid with a childhood
littered with bigger monsters than you. i've been
beaten into a silence more times than i've been
embraced on this earth. you haven't seen what i've
seen. my rock bottom went so deep i'm pretty sure it
was hell. i spent a decade climbing out of it. my hands
blistered. my feet swelled. my mind said *i can't take
it anymore.* i told my mind *you better get yourself
together. we came here for joy. and we are going
to feel all of it.* i've been hunted. killed. and walked
back to earth. i snapped the neck off every beast that
thought it could. and you want to take my seat. the
one i built with the story of my life. honey. you won't
fit. i juggle clowns like you. i pick my teeth with fools
like you for fun. i have played and slept and danced
with bigger devils.

on days you can't hear yourself
slow down to
let your mind and body
catch up to each other

- *stillness*

what a relief
to discover that
the aches i thought
were mine alone
are also felt by
so many others

my body renews itself in waves of ocean and blood

i have a very complicated relationship
with the country i was born in
our men were
slaughtered in those streets
our women were raped
while thousands were tortured
and disappeared by police
the indian state denies what they did
but no amount of yoga or bollywood
can make us forget the
sikh genocide they orchestrated

- never forget 1984

i will never be quiet
about the way my
people resisted
so i could be free

our wounds are the reason
i started writing poetry
every word
i've ever written was to
lead us back into our arms

they could take away
everything we have
and we'd conjure this
beautiful life up all over again
with the bones in our backs
building an empire
from the ground up
is exactly what we're good at

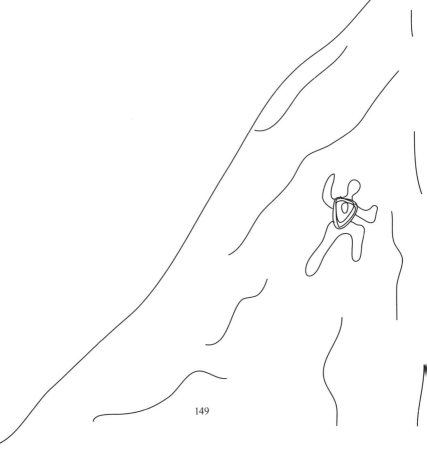

ours must be
a politic of revolution
freedom can't exist
until the most disadvantaged are free

don't sleep on
the doormat of your potential
waiting for things to happen
when you could *be*
the thing that happens

you are one person
but when you move
an entire community
walks through you

- *you go nowhere alone*

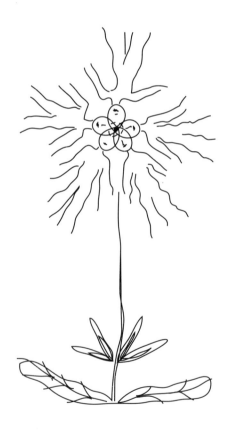

by virtue of living
in a racist world
nonblack people are
raised to be antiblack
we are all taught that
lighter is better

- *undoing*

your voice
is your sovereignty

- *free*

you look tired he says
i turn to him and say
yeah i'm exhausted
i've been fighting misogyny for decades
how else do you expect me to look

no one on this planet
is in more denial
than the white man
who regardless of all
the evidence in front of him
still thinks racism and sexism
and all the world's pain don't exist

the world is changing
can you feel it
undressing itself and slipping into
something uncomfortable
and more just

- *waves*

i'm not interested
in a feminism that thinks
simply placing women at the top
of oppressive systems is progress

- not your convenient figurehead

the future
world of our dreams
can't be built on the
corruptions of the past

- *tear it down*

today i saw myself for the first time
when i dusted off
the mirror of my mind
and the woman looking back
took my breath away
who was this beautiful beastling
this extra-celestial earthling
i touched my face and my reflection
touched the woman of my dreams
all her gorgeous smirking back at me
my knees surrendered to the earth
as i wept and sighed at how
i'd gone my whole life
being myself
but not seeing myself
spent decades living inside my body
never left it once
yet managed to miss all its miracles
isn't it funny how you can
occupy a space without
being in touch with it
how it took so long for me
to open the eyes of my eyes
embrace the heart of my heart
kiss the soles of my swollen feet
and hear them whisper
thank you
thank you
thank you
for noticing

you have everything to gain
from believing in yourself
yet you spend all your time with self-doubt

there is a conversation
happening inside you
pay deep attention
to what your inner world
is saying

i stopped resisting
the unpleasant feelings
and accepted that happiness
has nothing to do with
feeling good all the time

- *balance*

it's easy to love
the nice things about ourselves
but true self-love is
embracing the difficult parts
that live in all of us

- *acceptance*

can you hear the women who came before me
five hundred thousand voices
ringing through my neck
as if this were all a stage built for them
i can't tell which parts of me are me
and which parts are them
can you see them taking over my spirit
shaking out of my limbs
to do everything
they couldn't do
when they were alive

i dive into the well of my body
and end up in another world
everything i need
already exists in me
there's no need
to look anywhere else

- *home*

oh but the pussy is brave
lest we forget
how much pain
the pussy can take
how much pleasure it delivers
unto itself and others
remember
how it spit you out
without a flinch
now here you are
using the word *pussy*
like an insult
when you're not even
strong enough to be one

live loud and proud like you deserve
and reject their bullshit definition
of what a woman should look like

women have been starved of space for so long
when one of us finally
makes it into the arena
we get scared that another woman
will take our spot
but space doesn't work like that
look at all the men in the arena getting stronger
as their numbers multiply
more women in the arena means
more room for all of us to rise

- *stronger together*

i am not interested in a feminism
that excludes trans women

he says *you're opinionated*
as if it's an insult
to have ideas so big
he chokes on the size of them

- *never be quiet*

look for the women in the room
who have less space than you
listen
hear them
and act on what they're saying

- *amplify indigenous. trans. black. brown.*
  women of color voices.

why escape yourself
when you are so beautiful
get closer to your shine

on days i could not move
it was women
who came to water my feet
until i was strong enough
to stand
it was women
who nourished me
back to life

- *sisters*

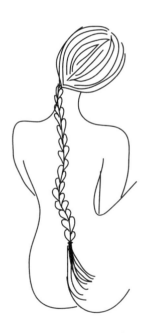

make it a point
to love yourself
as fiercely as you do other people

- *commitment*

it shouldn't affect anyone
what we do with our bodies
least of all those who haven't
walked a day in our shoes

give me laugh lines and wrinkles
i want proof of the jokes we shared
engrave the lines into my face like
the roots of a tree that grow deeper
with each passing year
i want sunspots as souvenirs
for the beaches we laid on
i want to look like i was
never afraid to let the world
take me by the hand
and show me what it's made of
i want to leave this place knowing
i did something with my body
other than trying to
make it look perfect

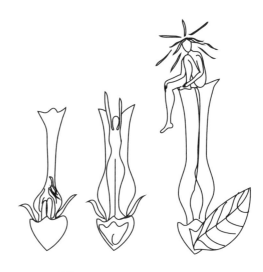

i can't take my eyes off of me
now that i see myself
i can't take my mind off of me
can't believe the tricks
my hands have been up to
the sermons i spoke into existence
the mountains i crushed
with my fingers
and the mountains i built
from all the shit
people tried to
stone me to death with

- *warrior*

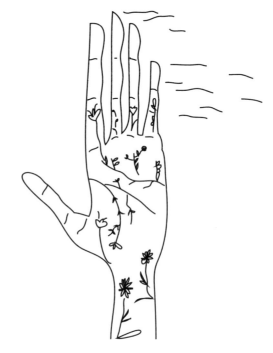

i often daydream about the woman i'll be
when i leave the rush of
my insecure twenties
and pick up self-assurance on the way
i can't wait to make
my eighteen-year-old self jealous
of the hell i raise
roaring into my thirties and forties
my soul becoming
more potent with age
at fifty i'll sit with
my wrinkles and silver hair
laughing about the adventures
we've had together
talking about the countless more
in the decades ahead
what a privilege it is
to grow into the
finest version of myself

- *aging*

be here
in what needs to be done today

- *that's how you honor tomorrow*

if the devil hadn't
pushed you into a corner
and forced you to break its neck
how would you have known
you were this strong

there are miracles in me
waiting their turn to happen
i am never giving up on myself

you do not belong to the future or the past

- *you belong right here*

get loud
say what you need to say
it feels good to reclaim your life

the way we rise
from every sorrow in life
is the most gorgeous thing i've seen

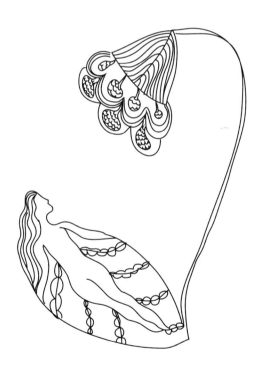

you are a soul. a world. a portal. a spirit. you are never alone. you are organs and blood and flesh and muscle. a colony of miracles weaving into each other.

break down
every door they built
to keep you out
and bring all your people with you

- *storm*

you are not alone
alone would be if
your heart no longer beat
and your lungs no longer pulled
and your breath no longer pushed
how are you alone if
an entire community lives in you

- *you have all of you on your side*

i will never have
this version of me again
let me slow down
and be with her

- *always evolving*

your beauty is undeniable
but everything sacred and ancient in you
is even more stunning

i am waking up to my godself

nothing tastes better than
being on your own side

i'm not afraid of failing
i'm afraid my potential
might set the world on fire

there are days
when the light flickers
and then i remember
i am the light
i go in and
switch it back on

- *power*

you have only scratched the surface
of what you're capable of
there are decades
of victories ahead of you

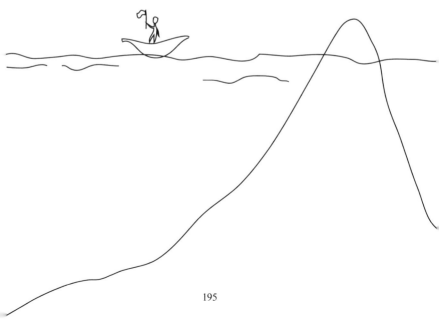

silly girl
little angel
little devil
so oblivious to
being the miracle worker
you are the mother
the magician
the master of your life

now that you are free
and the only obligation you are under
is your own dreams
what will you do
with your time

extra sugar
for this edition

the power of knowing your worth is
you never run out of reasons to love yourself

maybe the void
isn't meant to be filled
and parts of me are
supposed to remain wanting

in the darkest times
i've seen us become our brightest
standing on balconies and
singing to the empty streets below us
we manage to crack jokes in the saddest times
sometimes it takes a crisis to remember
our lives depend on each other
and we will end up nowhere if we try to go alone

i miss my old brain
before my phone
was attached to my wrist
and social media became the place
i was most social
i miss having all that extra space
in my head to stretch out
and be imaginative
instead
i'm full of
information about
people i don't know
i miss what it felt like to live
before the internet
before instagram
before my online persona
became the real me

everyone has their truth
the eyes through which
they see the world
the truth they think
they're experiencing
and then
there is the truth that
belongs to reality
the eternal
unbiased truth
that picks no sides
the one we cannot see
cause we are blinded by
our own version of the story

- *perception*

poems
illustrations
and cover art by:

rupi kaur

other books by rupi kaur:

milk and honey

the sun and her flowers

rupi kaur is a poet. artist. and performer. as a 21-year-old university student rupi wrote. illustrated. and self-published her first poetry collection *milk and honey*. next came its artistic sibling *the sun and her flowers*. these collections have sold over 8 million copies and have been translated into over 40 languages. *home body* is her third collection of poetry. rupi's work touches on love. loss. trauma. healing. femininity. and migration. she feels most at home when creating art or performing her poetry onstage. learn more at www.rupikaur.com.

Andrews McMeel Publishing
a division of Andrews McMeel Universal
1130 Walnut Street, Kansas City, Missouri 64106

www.andrewsmcmeel.com
www.rupikaur.com

21 22 23 24 25 SDB 10 9 8 7 6 5 4 3 2 1

ISBN: 978-1-5248-6967-0

Library of Congress Control Number: 2021941039

Illustrations and cover design by Rupi Kaur

MIX
Paper from
responsible sources
FSC® C144853

ATTENTION: SCHOOLS AND BUSINESSES
Andrews McMeel books are available at quantity discounts with bulk purchase
for educational, business, or sales promotional use. For information, please
e-mail the Andrews McMeel Publishing Special Sales Department:
specialsales@amuniversal.com.